IDEO OOK

ARLEN ROTH TEACHES
SLIDE GUITAR

T0088786

Cover Photo by Diana Dickinson

To access video visit:
www.halleonard.com/mylibrary

Enter Code
2161-0887-1849-3623

ISBN 978-1-4950-6283-4

HAL•LEONARD®

7777 W. BLUEMOUND RD. P.O. BOX 13819 MILWAUKEE, WI 53213

In Australia Contact:
Hal Leonard Australia Pty. Ltd.
4 Lentara Court
Cheltenham, Victoria, 3192 Australia
Email: ausadmin@halleonard.com.au

Visit Hal Leonard Online at
www.halleonard.com

CONTENTS

OPEN G TUNING

STANDARD TUNING

INTRODUCTION

Slide guitar has long been one of my favorite styles to play, but I've also been teaching it for almost as long as I could play it! In fact, I believe that my first experience with the guitar in general was sliding around on my brother's guitar, which had only two strings left on it, using my mother's lipstick cover. I would play it on my lap, not only because that seemed to make the most sense, but I had probably been watching steel guitar players on TV as a kid, such as Alvino Ray and others. This was when I was only six or seven years old, so I was just playing around and thought slide guitar looked easy to do!

About the Video

Each chapter in the book includes a full video lesson, so you can see and hear the material being taught. To access all of the videos that accompany this book, simply visit **www.halleonard.com/mylibrary** and enter the code found on page 1. The music examples that include video demonstrations are marked with an icon throughout the book, and the timecode listed with each icon tells you exactly where on the video the example is performed.

CHAPTER 1

At least for me, slide has always seemed to make a lot of sense, and I have always managed to fall into many of the right habits and techniques over the years. For example, when I wrote my first and very successful book, *Slide Guitar* (distributed by Hal Leonard), I was just 19! I can recall saying to myself, "How is it that I know all of this stuff on slide guitar?" After all, nobody was around to show me anything at all, and visual clues about slide playing were pretty few and far between in those days!

I certainly had the good fortune to start at the age of 10 with some classical guitar lessons down in Greenwich Village, during which my teacher instilled in me a great respect for the right hand and its role in being "dedicated" to the strings correctly. I also learned just how important dampening (or muting) the strings with the right hand really is! So in this chapter, we're going to cover the basics of using the slide before we delve into the licks.

Which Type of Slide?

What slide we choose has a lot to do with what kind of tone we end up creating. The most common choices we have for slides are glass, brass, chrome, other metals, and ceramic. I have always gravitated towards a brass slide with a lot of weight. I feel that this gives me the best tone and the kind of sustain I look for in slide guitar. Glass can work pretty well, especially on acoustic guitar, but it tends to be uneven in tone and sustain; somehow it always lets me down. If you do use glass, make sure it's rather thick and has good weight for sustain. Ceramic has a good and interesting tone and should not be overlooked. Shiny chrome is just too "slick" and lacks the grit of a brass slide, which can help get that dirty, scratchy sound we all love so much—especially when we play with the all-important technique of vibrato. So for me, heavy brass works best in both electric and acoustic applications.

Now let's get to some right-hand technique! Before we do, though, let's get into open D tuning, which is one of the most common slide tunings of all. The notes, low to high, are:

 (5:30)   D–A–D–F♯–A–D

Dampening and Muting

The right hand (plucking hand) is far and away the most important element to slide guitar playing. We must work even harder to eliminate excess sounds than when playing standard guitar, due to the fact that we have a foreign object on our fretting hand.

If you've ever observed a really good slide player, such as Bonnie Raitt, Lee Roy Parnell, Derek Trucks, or Ry Cooder, you can see that the right hand is usually working overtime to make sure we're only hearing the strings that are intended to sound. For example, if you want to play only the B string, which would usually be plucked by the middle finger, the ring finger would be muting the high E string, while the thumb would be muting the bottom four strings. I like to refer to this as the thumb "letting a string breathe." So if there's a lick using the high E and B strings, and suddenly the G string is needed, the thumb simply drops down one more string towards the low E, allowing that G string to now "breathe."

Take the following lick, for example. The thumb begins by laying across (muting) strings 6–2 and slowly works its way back across the strings as we descend. The unused fingers mute the higher strings.

 (11:21)

EXAMPLE 1

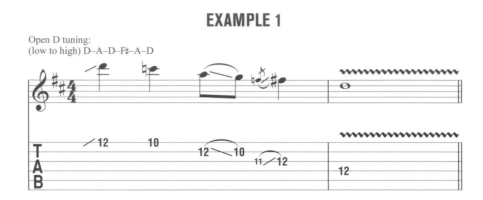

It's a hard thing to do in a non-instinctive way, and therefore a hard thing to teach, but I simply stumbled upon this when I was first starting to play slide. For some reason, I always seemed to take the correct approach. I can recall having to dissect this technique so I could explain it in my first book, and also when I started teaching slide to private students and in workshops. It almost made me a little too "technique-conscious" when I played during that time, and I had to make sure to allow myself to become more "unconscious" again when it came to my natural approach to slide, which I did not want to adversely affect!

As you can see in the video, the right hand's involvement is really key to proper muting, and the two specific ways that exist depend on which direction the lick is headed in! Simply put, if the notes are moving towards the high E string, the thumb is what isolates the higher strings from the lower; it also determines which strings get to breathe, regardless of the direction. If the lick is being played by the index, middle, and ring fingers, those three fingers act as a group, always moving in threes. Therefore, if you are playing the top three strings and then need to introduce the D (fourth) string, those three fingers will move over to cover the D, G, and B strings. This will become second nature after a while. Also remember that, as that fourth string is introduced, the thumb muting simultaneously allows it to open up and breathe. Also, and equally important, if we want to introduce a new string as we move towards the low E, the very finger that played the string is the same one that dampens it out as the new string is played.

The main thing that we are stressing here is that, of course, when playing slide, many notes and strings tend to over-sustain and mush together. Sometimes this is desirable, but often times it's not, and many wrong notes and overtones can occur. The art of playing slide and truly articulating the notes individually is what we all should aim for, and this is what muting is all about!

Playing with a Pick?

If you play with a pick, you are right away creating a disadvantage for yourself with slide. As you know, when you are flatpicking, you can almost never play notes truly simultaneously. You'll also have to rely on the picking hand to dampen unwanted strings in a far more unconventional way than if you are fingerpicking. Flatpicking orients you much more towards single-note playing as well, with far fewer double- and triple-stops available to you. Any extra notes you'd need would have to be additionally picked or may require you to "jump over" some strings to get to, and this can also get to be rather tedious and tiring after a while.

Let's face it: fingerstyle is the way to go for slide, and you'll find it much more rewarding, even though you'll have to definitely put in the time to practice and make it work. Playing slide using a flatpick will get very boring and repetitious after a while, and in the end you'd want to switch over to fingerstyle anyway!

The Blues Box Scale Positions in Open D

Once you've gotten fairly adept at the whole muting and dampening deal, it's time to put that to the test with some single-note scales, positions, and runs. The reason I call these "box" positions is that you immediately start to recognize the shapes that these scales make, and it becomes easier and easier to naturally fall into these positions as we begin to improvise in blues and other genres.

This is all based on the two main pentatonic scales we are equally aware of in normal guitar playing: the minor and major pentatonics. Here we'll look at the minor or "blues" pentatonic. As you know, when you bend strings, you are not only going from one note to another; you're also playing "through" many other microtones that exist on the way from one note to another. I personally love working this kind of sound when I play, and it's something that is purely connected to the musical soul of the player. It's definitely the most vocal-like style of all forms of guitar playing. Well, this also applies very much to slide guitar playing. Not only can you feel and hear those "in between" notes, but in the case of the slide over the frets, you can also visualize and actually see where the notes are being played. That combination of being able to hear, see, and feel all at the same time is something really unique to slide guitar, for sure!

The higher up closed (fretted) blues box position can be very efficient, as it basically uses two frets for the most part, with just a couple of notes that go beyond the boundaries of the box. Again, even though all of its notes are closed, there are other places for those same notes in the same octaves as well!

 (12:22)

EXAMPLE 2

Open D tuning:
(low to high) D–A–D–F#–A–D

7

Notice that, in the previous example, I'm sliding from the minor 3rd (F) to the major 3rd in both octaves. Although the minor pentatonic scale is technically spelled 1–♭3–4–5–♭7 and therefore contains a minor 3rd, it's extremely common in blues to grace into the major 3rd. This is why it's sometimes also called the "blues pentatonic."

The open position of the minor pentatonic uses many open-string notes that can also be found on the frets as well. This gives you enormous flexibility down low, and the sound of answering an open note with a fretted version of the same note (sometimes with vibrato too) can give a lovely "before and after" kind of sound that's often used by many standard guitarists playing blues or rock guitar. When I illustrate this open blues scale, you'll see how I make sure to illustrate those open as well as closed notes. This is one of the great things about being a stringed instrument player. As opposed to a fixed-note instrument like piano, we can find many places to play the exact same note!

In this example, I'll play the strict minor pentatonic scale—using the minor 3rd (F) throughout—so you can hear the difference. Compare this to the higher position that we previously covered.

 (13:10)

EXAMPLE 3

Open D tuning:
(low to high) D–A–D–F♯–A–D

An alternative version of the same scale could make use of more open strings, like this:

EXAMPLE 4

Open D tuning:
(low to high) D–A–D–F♯–A–D

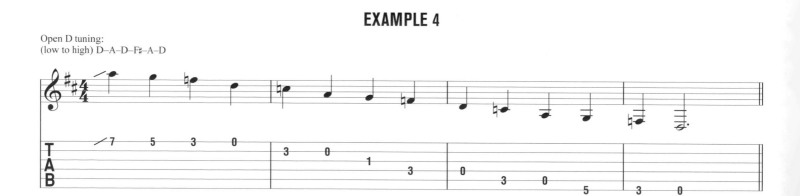

CHAPTER 2

The Major Pentatonic Scale in Open D

In more of a country-style blues, the major pentatonic is commonly used instead of (or in addition to) the minor pentatonic. This scale is spelled 1–2–3–5–6. It's still five notes (*penta* meaning five), but it's a different set of five notes than the minor pentatonic.

Here's an open position form of D major pentatonic.

 (0:58)

EXAMPLE 1

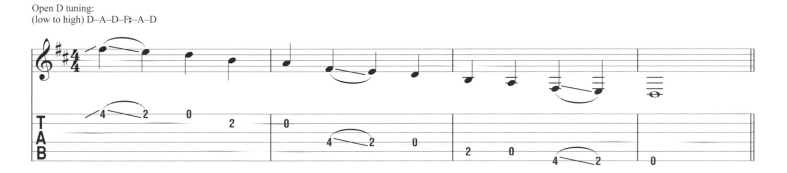

In an open position like this, there is a very subtle technique I use in which I actually tilt, or arch, the slide so I can play along with the curvature of the neck. This allows some open strings to be played while there are fretted harmony notes as well. You'll see the importance of using only as much of the slide as is needed, and how the pinky needs to just stick out of the slide enough so it can sense where the edge of the slide actually is! This is very critical to accurate playing, because, as I stated earlier, we're already dealing with a foreign object on our finger, so we need to clean up the sound as much as possible!

By tilting the slide in this way, we can, for example, play slide on the first string while still allowing other open strings to ring.

 (1:51)

EXAMPLE 2

9

This idea can be really fleshed out to create some Dobro-sounding ideas. Here's an example that uses mostly the I chord (D), but there are a few V chords (A) and one IV chord (G) as well. Notice that I voice the V chord with two open strings (5 and 2) and one slide note (fret 2, string 1), but the IV chord is played entirely with the slide. For the pull-off in measure 3, just touch the note with the slide and then quickly "zing" it off the string (see the video).

 (3:07)

EXAMPLE 3

Hammer-Ons

To perform a hammer-on with the slide, simply pluck the open string and then bring the slide down onto the string at the desired location. You don't have to slam it down; only use enough force needed to sound the note.

 (3:55)

EXAMPLE 4

What's equally important here, however, is the right hand. You have to make sure that only the string you're hammering on is allowed to sound, otherwise you'll hear the slide hammering down on all the strings it comes in contact with. This means, in the above example, laying the thumb across strings 6–3 and muting string 1 with an unused plucking finger.

Playing Harmonies in Open D

One of the biggest benefits of playing slide in open tunings is the ability to play chords and harmonies with the slide. Again, right-hand muting is paramount here. You want to make sure that only the strings you're plucking are allowed to sound (unless you're specifically going for more of a messy sound).

Take this little riff, for example.

 (5:15)

EXAMPLE 5

At first, my ring finger is muting the high E string while my thumb is muting strings 6–4. I pluck the notes on strings 3–2 with my index and middle fingers, respectively. Then, when I move to strings 4–3, my ring finger moves over to mute string 2.

You can get some Hawaiian-type sounds by doing this.

 (5:38)

EXAMPLE 6

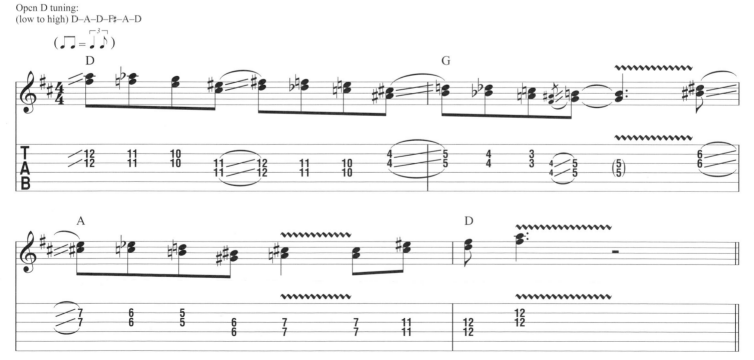

When you combine this idea with some right-hand fingerpicking patterns, you can get some really cool things. Here's a riff from my song "Tumblin'," which is from my album *Toolin' Around Woodstock* with Levon Helm. We're sticking to the bass strings almost exclusively here, so I assign my thumb to string 6, index to string 5, middle to string 4, and ring to string 3.

 (6:38)

EXAMPLE 7

Open D tuning:
(low to high) D–A–D–F♯–A–D

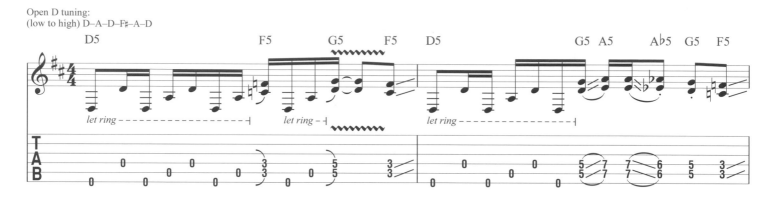

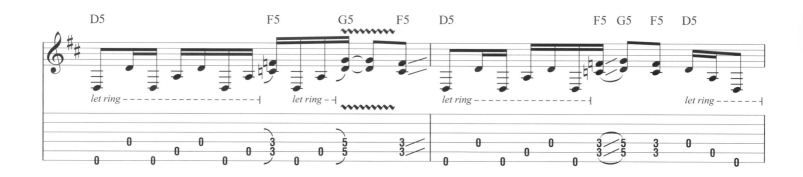

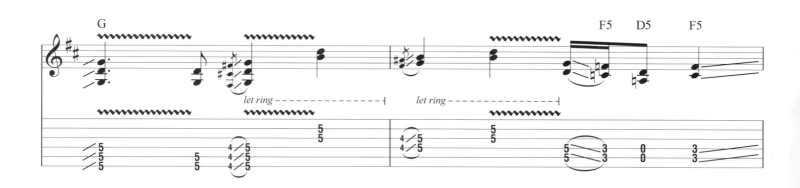

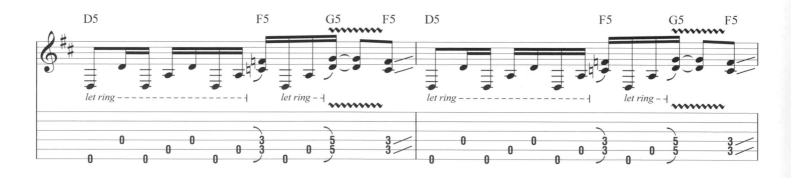

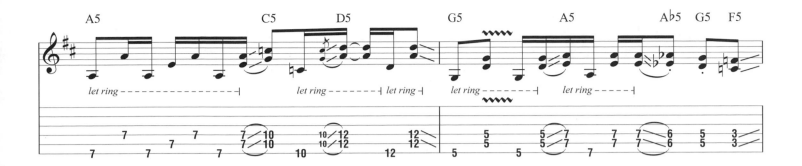

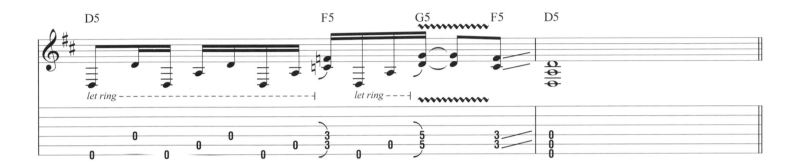

Reminder: Over the Fret Wire!

It never hurts to remind players that, in order to play slide properly in tune, you need to position the slide directly over the fret wire–not in between two frets, as is the case when we fret a guitar with standard technique. If you do that, you'll sound flat. So remember to align the slide directly over the fret wire, and you'll be in good shape.

 (8:00)

CHAPTER 3

Angling the Slide

In the very early days of slide guitar, people like Blind Willie Johnson would often just keep an alternating bass going and then double the vocal melody on the first string with the slide. This is great practice with angling the slide, as we briefly discussed earlier.

Here's an example of that kind of idea.

 (0:30)

EXAMPLE 1

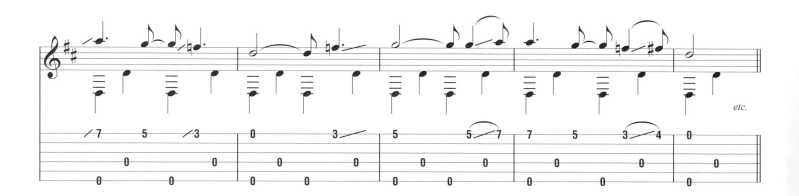

Again, you have to remember to keep the slide angled so that it's only making contact with the first string. This will allow you to play the other open strings as well if you'd like.

Perpendicular Please

This sort of goes along with the concept of aligning the slide over the fret wire. When you're playing more than one note, make sure the slide is perpendicular to the guitar neck so that all of the notes you play are in tune. If you make it a habit to always align your slide along the length of the fret wire, this will become second nature to you. Nevertheless, it's always good to check yourself when you're playing a chord to make sure the slide is perpendicular.

There is one exception to this, and that's when we want to play different intervals and actually need to angle the slide to accomplish this. For example, in this line, we're descending the D major scale (with some chromatic passing tones) in 6ths on strings 1 and 3. The problem is that some of the intervals are major 6ths and others are minor 6ths. The minor 6ths at the beginning are easy because those two strings are tuned that way in open D; so you just keep the slide perpendicular. In order to get the minor 6ths intervals, however, you need to angle the slide so that you hit one fret higher on string 1 than you do on string 3.

 (2:22)

EXAMPLE 2

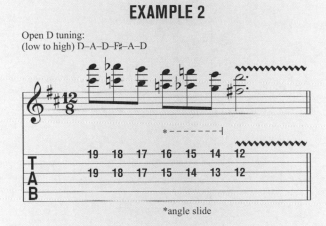

*angle slide

It takes a bit of practice, but it is doable!

Playing Chords in Open D

When we change tunings, obviously our chord shapes will change as well. So let's take a look at some chord shapes in open D.

Of course, the I chord, D, can't get any easier; it's played with all open strings.

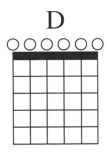

D

The IV chord, G, can be played like this, as a colorful add9 chord:

 (3:35)

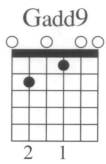

Or if you add the second fret on string 2, you get a standard G major chord:

 (3:53)

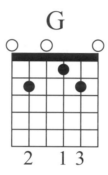

A ii chord, Em, can be played like this:

 (4:06)

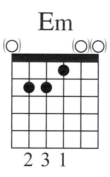

The notes in parentheses in the grids are optional color notes.

And move that up two frets for the iii chord, F♯m:

 (4:14)

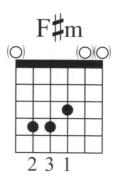

The V chord, A, looks like this:

 (4:25)

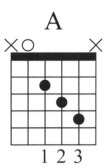

You can also play an A7 chord, without the 3rd (C♯), like this:

 (4:56)

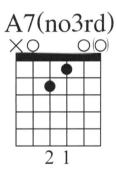

The ♭VII chord, C, looks like this:

 (5:08)

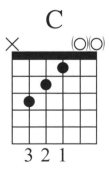

Playing Slide Fills in Open D

Once you get the basics of playing riffs and chords down, it's nice to be able to add some slide fills in the "dead spots" to keep the momentum going. Note that, especially if you're playing by yourself, it's critical to play in time to maintain the groove.

Here are a few prime examples.

 (6:05)

EXAMPLE 3

These fills are a prime place to insert some octaves. In open D tuning, you can play octaves with the slide two ways: on the 6/4 string pair or the 4/1 string pair. Here's an example of the former, in which I'm using my thumb and index finger.

▶ (7:05)

EXAMPLE 4

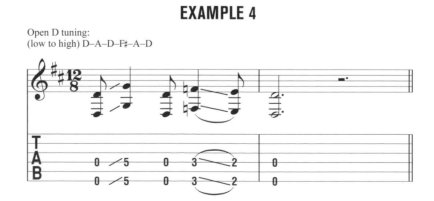

18

CHAPTER 4

Pull-Offs

We briefly mentioned pull-offs earlier, but let's look at them a little more closely here. To perform a pull-off with the slide, you can't just lift it straight off the string. It helps to give it a little "zing" either forward or backward.

 (0:54)

EXAMPLE 1

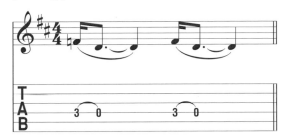

And here's a nice little pull-off lick on string 1.

 (3:38)

EXAMPLE 2

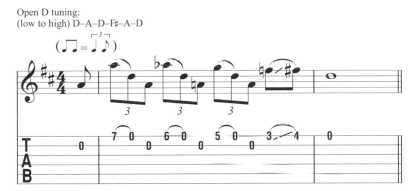

When you speed that one up, it's a bit difficult to zing off the string, but try to at least pull down a bit as you come off it.

Arpeggiating a Chord

To get a Hawaiian sound, we can use a technique in which we arpeggiate through a chord two notes at a time. Check it out here on a D chord.

 (4:22)

EXAMPLE 3

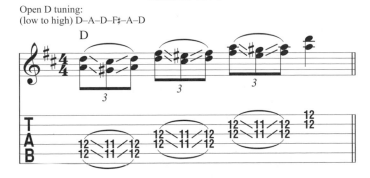

Or we can run straight up and down the chord without sliding around at all, like this A chord lick.

 (4:57)

EXAMPLE 4

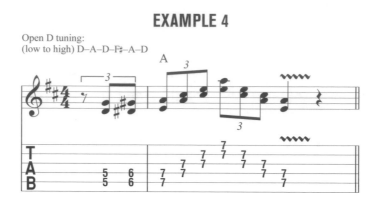

Harmonica-Style Licks in Open D

As a variation on the arpeggiation idea, you can create a harmonica-type sound by blurring through a chord and then "bending" down a note on top with the slide, imitating the classic move that's done on a harmonica.

 (5:30)

EXAMPLE 5

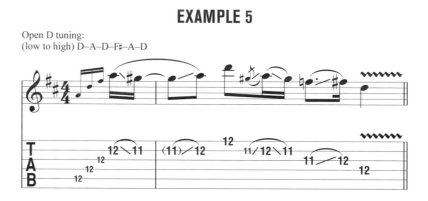

And then there's the classic grace-note lick that was used prominently by Duane Allman, among many others. Again, right-hand dampening is critical on this lick; otherwise it sounds like a mess! So while plucking string 2 with your middle finger, you need to be dampening string 3 with the index finger. While plucking string 3 with the index, you need to dampen string 2 with the middle. And the whole time, you're keeping the bass strings quiet with the thumb.

 (6:20)

EXAMPLE 6

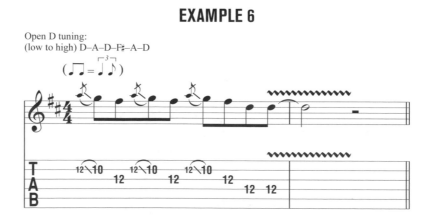

CHAPTER 5

Of course, all of these techniques will apply to slide guitar, regardless of your tuning preferences. I've always used the open E or open D configuration as my fundamental tuning, and I think it's a great starting point for most slide players. I suppose it is mostly because it relates so closely to standard guitar tuning, with only three strings re-tuned to form what we can easily picture as the E chord shape. It also creates some really nice harmonies and keeps two E notes and one B (in the case of open E) exactly where they were before we changed the tuning of the guitar. This keeps our ideas closely rooted to where they may have been in standard tuning. But now it's time to venture out to new slide tuning territory.

Open G Tuning

When discussing the other most popular tuning for slide, open G tuning, we now have another chord shape in common with standard tuning, but it's based on the three open strings (D, G, and B) that define an open G chord. So, to make open G work, we must lower our E strings as well as our A string a whole step. This does create an open G chord, but one that we are not as used to visualizing as we are in open E.

Some of the problems it can create are:

- Your high "root" note now exists on the fifth fret of string 1.
- Because the strings are more "slack" than before, open-position slides can get a bit "buzzy" and sloppy.
- String 6 (now tuned to D) is a low 5th, which many folks don't have a good use for (Keith Richards often cuts off his low E and plays with only five strings!). There are, however, many solutions better than eliminating a string!

So first let's move from open D tuning to open G tuning.

 (0:20)   **D–G–D–G–B–D**

Open G in D?

One time when I was working on a book with Ry Cooder, he explained to me how he uses G tuning very often for fingerpicking and slide, but his I chord is the D position, so therefore his IV chord becomes the open G. In other words, he plays in open G tuning but in the key of D. I love this approach, and it really taught me a lot when it came to understanding Ry's voicings. It also gave me a fresh outlook on how to utilize G tuning in not only a slide format, but also for non-slide guitar.

G tuning was, for a long time, the preferred tuning for the Delta blues out of Mississippi, and you hear it used to great effect by legends such as Son House, Robert Johnson, and Muddy Waters, just to name a few. In modern times, it's been well-utilized by greats such as Bonnie Raitt, Keith Richards (mostly for rhythm), and Lowell George (up to A tuning). I personally have used it in the A configuration, as in my version of "A Change Is Gonna Come" on my first album, *Guitarist*.

The Minor Pentatonic Scale in Open G

Let's check out some scale forms in our new open G tuning. The first will be the minor pentatonic.

 (2:45)

EXAMPLE 1

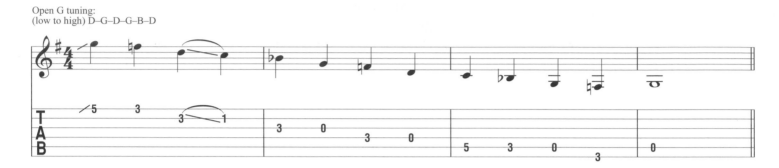

Check out the video for additional scale fingering options that you can use for more fretted notes in place of open strings.

The Major Pentatonic Scale in Open G

And here's a fingering for the major pentatonic.

 (3:36)

EXAMPLE 2

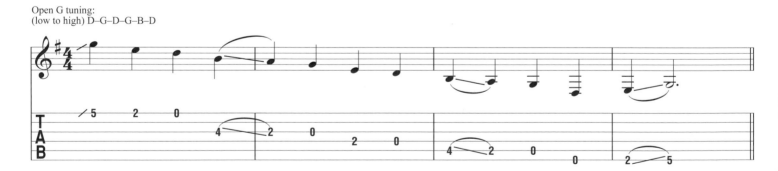

Playing Chords in Open G

Just as in the open E or open D tuning, it's very important to get to know your new chord positions—particularly the I, IV, and V. Of course, if you use the slide on the pinky as I recommend, you still have three fingers in a row that can more easily form chords than if you have the slide on your ring finger, or, God forbid, your second finger, as Ralph Macchio did when I coached him for the film *Crossroads*!

Let's check out some of our common chord shapes in open G now. Of course, our I chord, G, is all open.

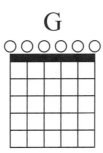

It's important to notice that, in open G, all of our intervals—this applies to licks, scales, and chords—are just moved over one string (toward the treble side) as compared to open D.

So here's our IV chord, C. If you include the optional open first string, you get a Cadd9 sound.

 (4:21)

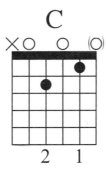

The V chord looks like this. Again, be sure to compare these to the open D forms to see the similarities.

 (4:42)

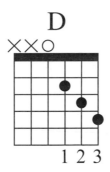

23

Playing Harmonies in Open G

Harmonies in open G are fairly similar to open D, but again, everything is moved up one string. We can use the slide-tilting technique to essentially re-create what Dobro players love to do when the guitar is placed on the lap. With many of these positions we are able to go from the I chord to the IV chord with a simple tilt of the slide, using our wrist to angle it and catch two notes on two different frets. Obviously, this becomes easier as we go up the neck, as the frets are closer to each other than in the lower fret positions.

 (5:04)

EXAMPLE 3

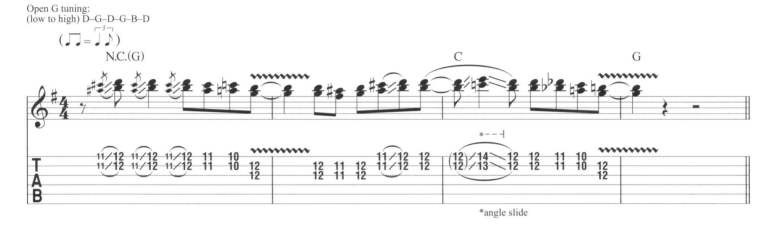

*angle slide

Blues Licks in Open G

Many of our blues licks can transfer nicely from open D when we keep in mind the "one-string over" trick. Here's an example of a lick that would normally be played on strings 2–4 in open D. In open G, it's played on strings 1–3.

 (6:36)

EXAMPLE 4

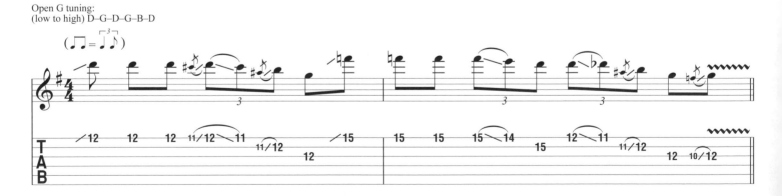

Regardless of how you intend to use this tuning though, it is firmly rooted in the early Delta blues styles that the founding fathers spoke so eloquently with!

CHAPTER 6

Standard Tuning

When I first started playing slide guitar, or any guitar for that matter, we had a cheap Stella guitar in the house that my brother brought back from college with only an E and a B string left on it. So what I used to do was, with my ear, tune the two strings in some kind of harmony to each other and start sliding away on them with my mom's lipstick holder. I was only about seven or eight years old, so I must've been emulating someone like Alvino Rey or Herb Remington, who I probably saw on TV. Where else would I get such an idea right off the bat?

I certainly had never even *held* a guitar with six strings yet, but maybe if I did, I would've tried playing slide in standard tuning, even though my first slide playing was definitely with open E tuning.

Now let's move from open G tuning to standard tuning.

 (0:44)   E–A–D–G–B–E

Standard tuning slide playing is fraught with danger, as there are very few easy "box positions" or chords that can be made, unless you really let yourself dig a lot deeper inside the possibilities and don't get too frustrated. It's far from what we like to think of as traditional slide guitar for sure, and we have way too many notes that need to be eliminated in order to get a clean slide approach. By far the biggest advantage to standard tuning is the ability to switch off between standard fretting and slide playing quickly. This can be a very handy technique, especially in a live performing situation!

Blues Pentatonic Scale Shape

Let's play a closed-position E blues pentatonic shape in standard tuning with the slide. If you thought right-hand dampening was important before, it's absolutely critical when playing in standard tuning, because it will sound like a total mess without it!

 (2:04)

EXAMPLE 1

The G-Form Chord Fragment

Remember, the guitar is now *not* tuned to a chord, so we can only hope for two or maybe three notes at any given time to harmonize when using the slide. There is at least one version of a box pattern, the most noteworthy being the three-note chord that is based on the open D, G, and B strings in a G chord. So, in other words, if we were playing in the key of E, this chord would be found at the ninth fret on strings 4–2. It's a good position for slide too, because it's high enough up the neck that we don't get too much buzzing.

 (2:48)

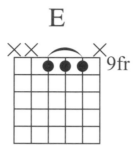

I can use this chord form to frame some licks and simulate—to a point—open tuning slide. So notice that, in the following lick, I use strict right-hand dampening until I reach that chord form, at which point I let the notes ring together to form the E chord.

 (3:00)

EXAMPLE 2

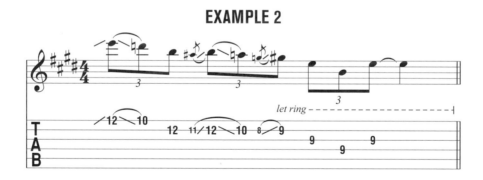

Using more chromatics can be helpful as well in standard tuning because it allows you to walk one note at a time along one string.

 (3:20)

EXAMPLE 3

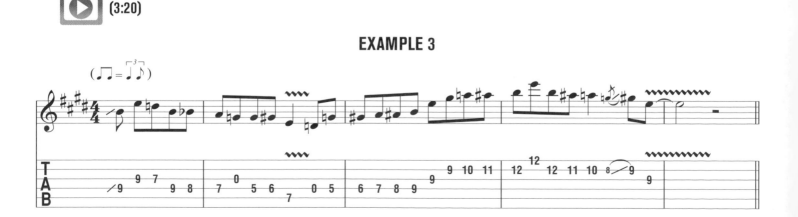

You can still simulate some open tuning-type licks, but it takes a bit more thought and precise execution.

(4:21)

EXAMPLE 4

Open Harmony in Standard Tuning

Although it's definitely not like open tuning, all is not lost in standard tuning regarding open harmony. You can still use the open B string and slide up to the G♯ at fret 4 on string 1 with the slide.

(4:48)

EXAMPLE 5

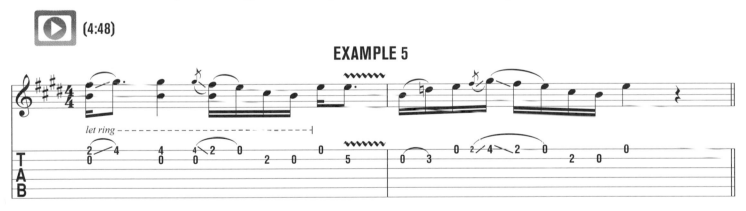

Below that, there's not too much available, but you do have the open low E string for your I chord and the open A string for the IV chord, which you can use if you're careful.

(4:57)

EXAMPLE 6

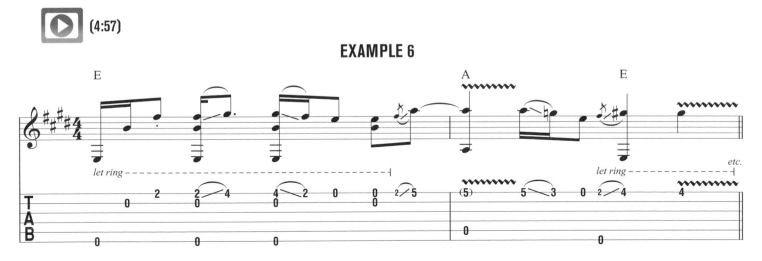

Minor Chords and Ninth Chords

Of course, just because we don't have a major chord available to us on the top strings doesn't mean we have to go without harmony up there completely. We *do* have a minor triad on strings 3–1, which can be used tastefully, although it's obviously not nearly as common. But it can still sound very nice.

 (5:55)

EXAMPLE 7

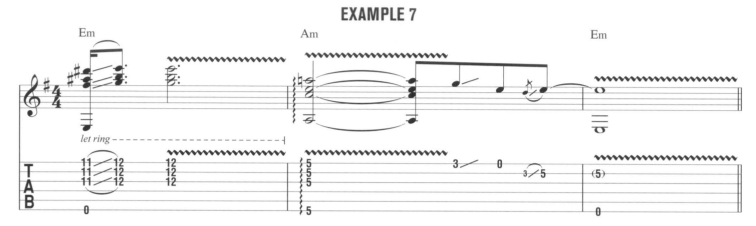

Of course, remember that we also have, for example, an E9 on the top three strings at the seventh fret. That Bm triad also masquerades as the top three notes of an E9 chord!

 (6:08)

E9

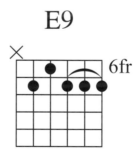

And if we move that three-string fragment up two frets, we get an E6.

 (6:21)

E6

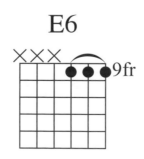

So, we can make use of those fragments, respective to the I, IV, and V chords, to navigate the chords of a blues.

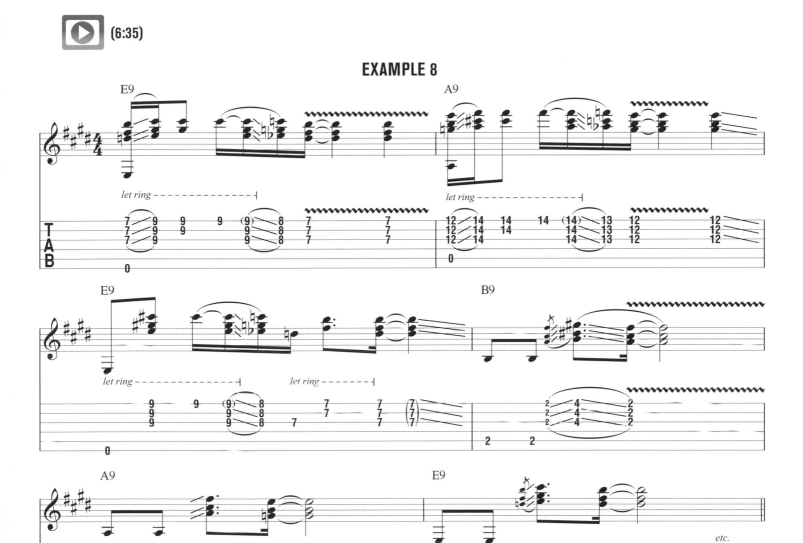

(6:35)

EXAMPLE 8

The Mick Method

Years ago, a few years after I had started the video side of Hot Licks Video, I had Mick Taylor, formerly of the Rolling Stones, do a guitar video for me that was largely based on slide playing. I was totally shocked as I saw him easily embrace two true "no-no's" of slide guitar: playing in standard tuning and using a *pick*! It's hard to believe, but if you study his approach, he uses a kind of "flat-picker's dampening," in which he employs the other fingers of the picking hand (middle, ring, and pinky) to come down behind the picked note in a kind of tapped motion. It's hard to describe, but it is much more of a standard guitar technique as opposed to one used in slide guitar!

So, you can try applying this Mick Taylor approach to standard tuning slide, but as you'll see in the video, I still prefer the good old right-hand fingerstyle approach for this, and the more traditional approach to dampening will certainly serve you well.

BONUS MATERIAL

"High Bass" G Tuning

This tuning is truly unique in the world of slide, but I felt it was important to shed some light on it for you. This is almost always used by Dobro players and has a unique layout in which the bottom three strings are tuned an octave lower than the top three strings: G–B–D–G–B–D. As you can probably imagine, this makes it very easy to play the same lick in two different octaves.

 (1:25)

EXAMPLE 1

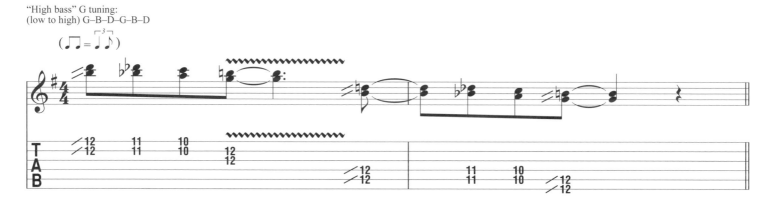

It can be a little confusing if you are already used to normal open G, especially because the lowest root note is switched from string 5 to string 6. Another thing I always found a bit strange was having such a low major 3rd (B) on string 5, but I eventually embraced the fact that I would have so many nice harmonies available to me, especially up the neck. It really helps you get around the neck, for closed positions mostly, but it's obviously great for open Dobro-like positions as well.

 (1:54)

EXAMPLE 2

This tuning has long been the favorite of all the early and contemporary greats, such as "Bashful" Brother Oswald, Josh Graves, Shot Jackson, Mike Auldridge, Cindy Cashdollar, and Jerry Douglas. That's not to say that this is the only tuning they prefer, but it certainly is mostly used for Dobro, and it's unusual to see it ever used for "upright" slide playing.

If you'd like to investigate the Dobro style more, I suggest checking out my *Beginning Dobro* video (distributed by Hal Leonard). It can help you understand this tuning and further "slide angling" techniques as well.

"Sonny Skies"

I used this tuning on a song I wrote for my *Slide Guitar Summit* album, which I recorded with the great Sonny Landreth. I called it "Sonny Skies" in his honor. I made deliberate use of all three bottom strings as bass notes—G, B, and D. This, along with the melody on top, helps define the chords as G, G7/B, and D.

Here's the basic idea for the riff:

 (3:27)

EXAMPLE 3

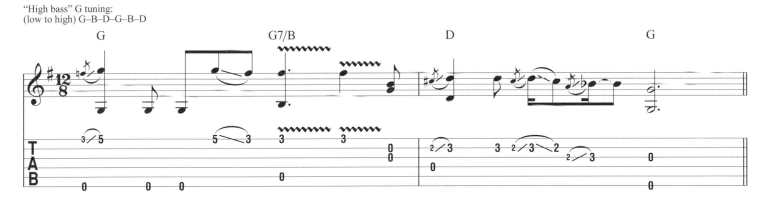

This tuning presents some really unique opportunities this way. Here's just a sampling of what can be done with this idea.

 (3:55)

EXAMPLE 4

"High bass" G tuning:
(low to high) G–B–D–G–B–D

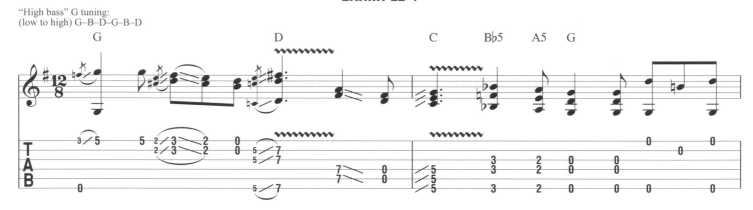

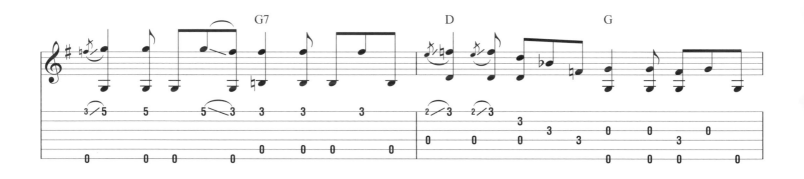

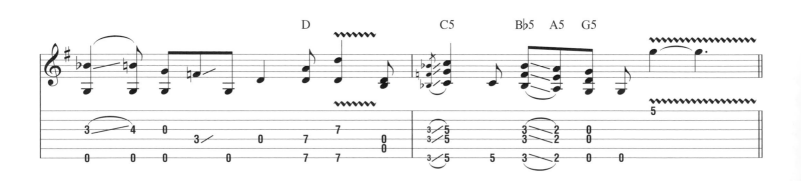

Power Chords in "High Bass" G Tuning

If you'll notice, I played the equivalent of a power chord a few times in the previous example, which is done by fretting strings 6, 4, and 3—skipping string 5.

 (6:19)

D5

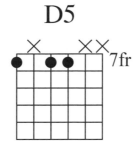

You can get some nice, powerful sounds with that shape.

 (6:38)

EXAMPLE 5

"High bass" G tuning:
(low to high) G–B–D–G–B–D

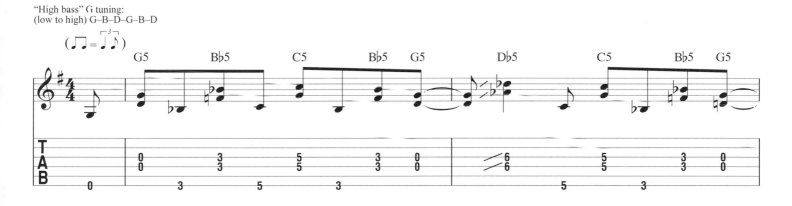

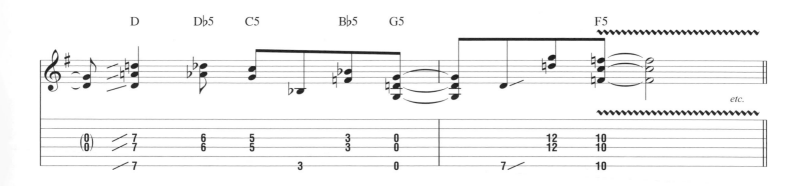

Open D Slide Guitar Jams

We'll close out with a couple of extended jams that tie together most of what we've talked about in this video book. I hope you enjoy.

▶ **OPEN D JAM #1**

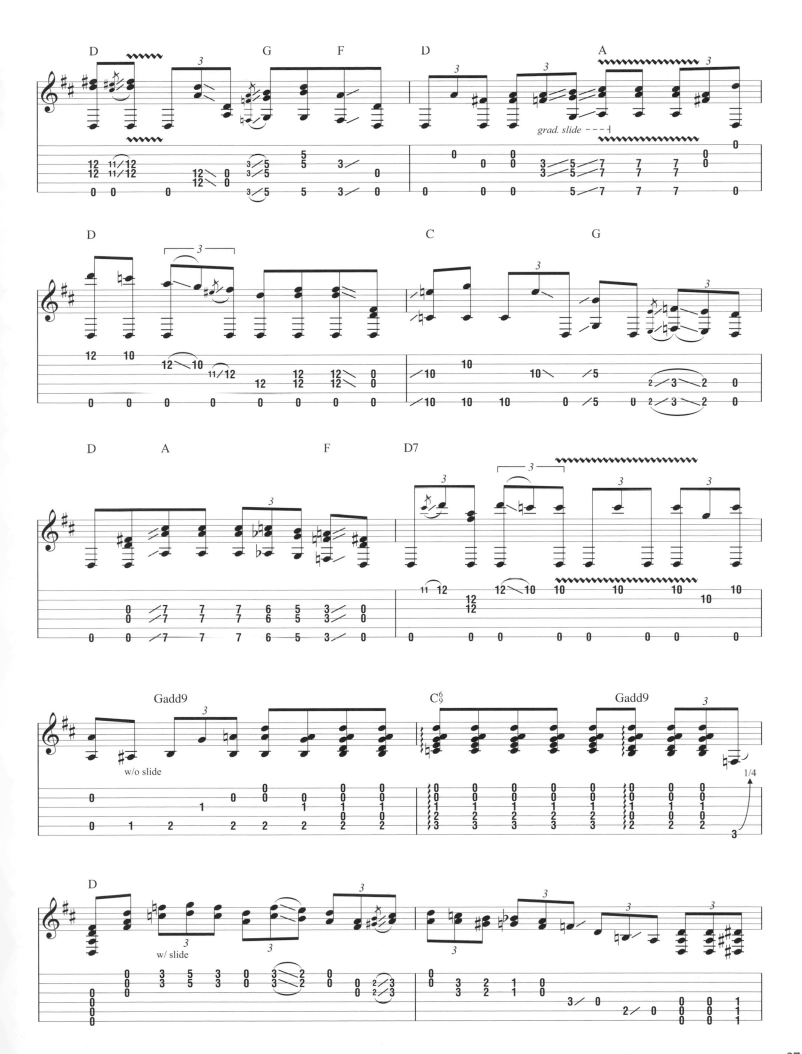

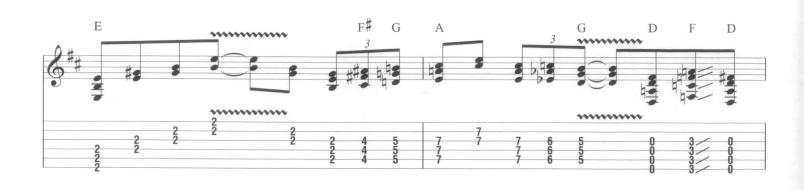

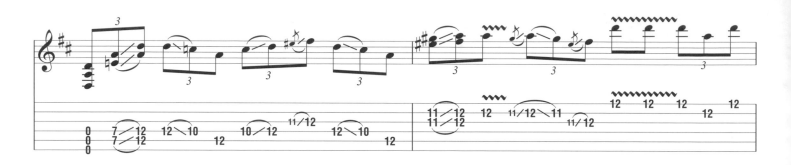

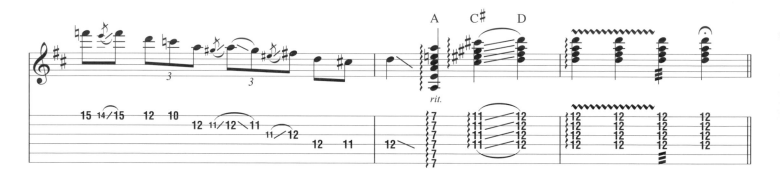

CONCLUSION

When it comes to slide guitar, I have tried to show you the many facets that make this art form so versatile and so expressive. From Delta blues to contemporary melodies, slide guitar has always proven to be among the most vocal-like and most evocative of almost all musical forms. And as you can see, fingerpicking is a very important aspect of slide guitar, if not the only way to play it.

I hope you have enjoyed these video lessons, and I look forward to seeing your innovations in the future, as we all continue to move on with these wonderful art forms within the infinite world of the guitar!

— Arlen Roth, 2017

Get Better at Guitar

...with these Great Guitar Instruction Books from Hal Leonard!

101 GUITAR TIPS
STUFF ALL THE PROS KNOW AND USE
by Adam St. James
This book contains invaluable guidance on everything from scales and music theory to truss rod adjustments, proper recording studio set-ups, and much more. The book also features snippets of advice from some of the most celebrated guitarists and producers in the music business, including B.B. King, Steve Vai, Joe Satriani, Warren Haynes, Laurence Juber, Pete Anderson, Tom Dowd and others, culled from the author's hundreds of interviews.
00695737 Book/Online Audio $16.99

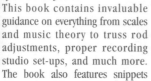

AMAZING PHRASING
50 WAYS TO IMPROVE YOUR IMPROVISATIONAL SKILLS
by Tom Kolb
This book/audio pack explores all the main components necessary for crafting well-balanced rhythmic and melodic phrases. It also explains how these phrases are put together to form cohesive solos. Many styles are covered – rock, blues, jazz, fusion, country, Latin, funk and more – and all of the concepts are backed up with musical examples. The companion audio contains 89 demos for listening, and most tracks feature full-band backing.
00695583 Book/Online Audio $19.95

BLUES YOU CAN USE – 2ND EDITION
by John Ganapes
This comprehensive source for learning blues guitar is designed to develop both your lead and rhythm playing. Includes: 21 complete solos • blues chords, progressions and riffs • turnarounds • movable scales and soloing techniques • string bending • utilizing the entire fingerboard • and more. This second edition now includes audio and video access online!
00142420 Book/Online Media.................................$19.99

FRETBOARD MASTERY
by Troy Stetina
Untangle the mysterious regions of the guitar fretboard and unlock your potential. *Fretboard Mastery* familiarizes you with all the shapes you need to know by applying them in real musical examples, thereby reinforcing and reaffirming your newfound knowledge. The result is a much higher level of comprehension and retention.
00695331 Book/Online Audio $19.99

FRETBOARD ROADMAPS – 2ND EDITION
ESSENTIAL GUITAR PATTERNS THAT ALL THE PROS KNOW AND USE
by Fred Sokolow
The updated edition of this bestseller features more songs, updated lessons, and a full audio CD! Learn to play lead and rhythm anywhere on the fretboard, in any key; play a variety of lead guitar styles; play chords and progressions anywhere on the fretboard; expand your chord vocabulary; and learn to think musically – the way the pros do.
00695941 Book/CD Pack...$14.95

GUITAR AEROBICS
A 52-WEEK, ONE-LICK-PER-DAY WORKOUT PROGRAM FOR DEVELOPING, IMPROVING & MAINTAINING GUITAR TECHNIQUE
by Troy Nelson
From the former editor of *Guitar One* magazine, here is a daily dose of vitamins to keep your chops fine tuned! Musical styles include rock, blues, jazz, metal, country, and funk. Techniques taught include alternate picking, arpeggios, sweep picking, string skipping, legato, string bending, and rhythm guitar. These exercises will increase speed, and improve dexterity and pick- and fret-hand accuracy. The accompanying audio includes all 365 workout licks plus play-along grooves in every style at eight different metronome settings.
00695946 Book/Online Audio $19.99

GUITAR CLUES
OPERATION PENTATONIC
by Greg Koch
Join renowned guitar master Greg Koch as he clues you in to a wide variety of fun and valuable pentatonic scale applications. Whether you're new to improvising or have been doing it for a while, this book/CD pack will provide loads of delicious licks and tricks that you can use right away, from volume swells and chicken pickin' to intervallic and chordal ideas. The CD includes 65 demo and play-along tracks.
00695827 Book/CD Pack...$19.95

INTRODUCTION TO GUITAR TONE & EFFECTS
by David M. Brewster
This book/CD pack teaches the basics of guitar tones and effects, with audio examples on CD. Readers will learn about: overdrive, distortion and fuzz • using equalizers • modulation effects • reverb and delay • multi-effect processors • and more.
00695766 Book/CD Pack...$14.99

PICTURE CHORD ENCYCLOPEDIA
This comprehensive guitar chord resource for all playing styles and levels features five voicings of 44 chord qualities for all twelve keys – 2,640 chords in all! For each, there is a clearly illustrated chord frame, as well as *an actual photo* of the chord being played! Includes info on basic fingering principles, open chords and barre chords, partial chords and broken-set forms, and more.
00695224...$19.95

SCALE CHORD RELATIONSHIPS
by Michael Mueller & Jeff Schroedl
This book teaches players how to determine which scales to play with which chords, so guitarists will never have to fear chord changes again! This book/audio pack explains how to: recognize keys • analyze chord progressions • use the modes • play over nondiatonic harmony • use harmonic and melodic minor scales • use symmetrical scales such as chromatic, whole-tone and diminished scales • incorporate exotic scales such as Hungarian major and Gypsy minor • and much more!
00695563 Book/Online Audio $14.99

SPEED MECHANICS FOR LEAD GUITAR
Take your playing to the stratosphere with the most advanced lead book by this proven heavy metal author. *Speed Mechanics* is the ultimate technique book for developing the kind of speed and precision in today's explosive playing styles. Learn the fastest ways to achieve speed and control, secrets to make your practice time really count, and how to open your ears and make your musical ideas more solid and tangible. Packed with over 200 vicious exercises including Troy's scorching version of "Flight of the Bumblebee." Music and examples demonstrated on CD. 89-minute audio.
00699323 Book/CD Pack...$19.95

TOTAL ROCK GUITAR
A COMPLETE GUIDE TO LEARNING ROCK GUITAR
by Troy Stetina
This unique and comprehensive source for learning rock guitar is designed to develop both lead and rhythm playing. It covers: getting a tone that rocks • open chords, power chords and barre chords • riffs, scales and licks • string bending, strumming, palm muting, harmonics and alternate picking • all rock styles • and much more. The examples are in standard notation with chord grids and tab, and the audio includes full-band backing for all 22 songs.
00695246 Book/Online Audio $19.99

Visit Hal Leonard Online at
www.halleonard.com

Prices, contents, and availability subject to change without notice.

0817